Investigate

Magnets

Charlotte Guillain

Heinemann Library
Chicago, Illinois

2008 Heinemann Library
a division of Capstone Global Library, LLC.
Chicago, Illinois

Customer Service 888-454-2279
Visit our website at www.heinemannraintree.com

Designed by Joanna Hinton-Malivoire Victoria Bevan, and Hart McLeod
Printed in the United States of America in North Mankato, Minnesota. 112012   007019RP

14 13 12
10 9 8 7 6 5 4 3 2 1

The Library of Congress has cataloged the first edition as follows:
Guillain, Charlotte.
 Magnets / Charlotte Guillain.
    p. cm. -- (Investigate)
 Includes bibliographical references and index.
 ISBN 978-1-4329-1391-5 (hc) -- ISBN 978-1-4329-1407-3 (pb) 1. Magnets--Juvenile literature. I. Title.
 QC753.7.G86 2008
 538'.4--dc22

                                  2008006809

Acknowledgments
The publishers would like to thank the following for permission to reproduce photographs: ©Alamy pp. **4** (Friedrich Saurer), **13** (ELC); ©Corbis pp. **11**, **29** (Sean Justice), **23** (Mark Ralston/Reuters), **25**, **26** Paul Seheult: Eye Ubiquitous); ©Getty Images pp. **24** (Andersen Ross/Blend Images), **28** (Joseph Van Os/Riser); ©istockphoto pp. **14** (Matthew Cole), **18** (Ina Peters); ©Pearson Education Ltd. pp. **5**, **17** (Tudor Photography), **6-10**, **12**, **15**, **16**, **19-21**, **30** (Lord and Leverett 2007); ©Science Photo Library p. **22** (Jeremy Walker); ©Ufuk ZIVANA/istockphoto p. **26**.

Cover photograph reproduced with permission of © Alamy (blickwinkel).

Contents

Some words are shown in bold, **like this**. You can find out what they mean by looking in the glossary.

What Are Magnets?

People use magnets every day. Magnets can pull each other together. They can also push each other away. Magnets can also push or pull other objects.

⬆ Some toys use magnets.

Magnets come in many different shapes and sizes. They can be used in many ways.

How Magnets Work

Magnets use a **force** that can pull other objects toward them. This force is called **magnetism**. A force is a push or a pull. When a magnet pulls objects we say it **attracts** them. Magnets do not attract all objects.

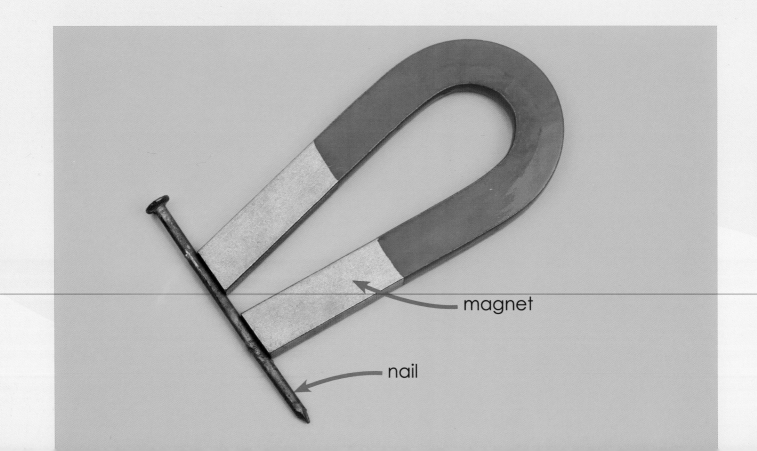

magnet

nail

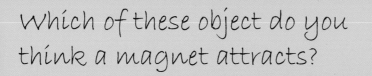
? **CLUES**

- The objects are hard.
- The objects are shiny.

7

A A magnet attracts metal objects such as paperclips. Magnets do not attract plastic, wood, glass, or any other materials.

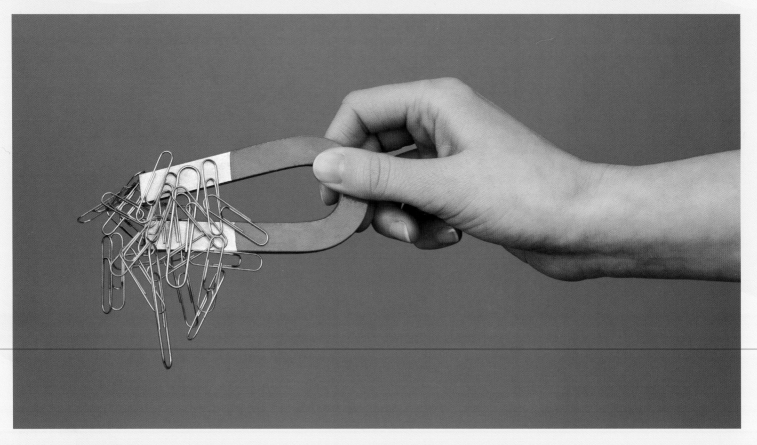

Magnets do not attract all metals. Magnets only attract objects made of certain metals such as iron, steel, and nickel. Cars, paper clips, refrigerators, washing machines, airplanes, and many other things are made of steel or iron.

A magnet would not attract this can because it is not made of iron.

Magnets have two ends or sides. These are called **poles**. A magnet has a north pole and a south pole. The north pole of one magnet attracts the south pole of another magnet.

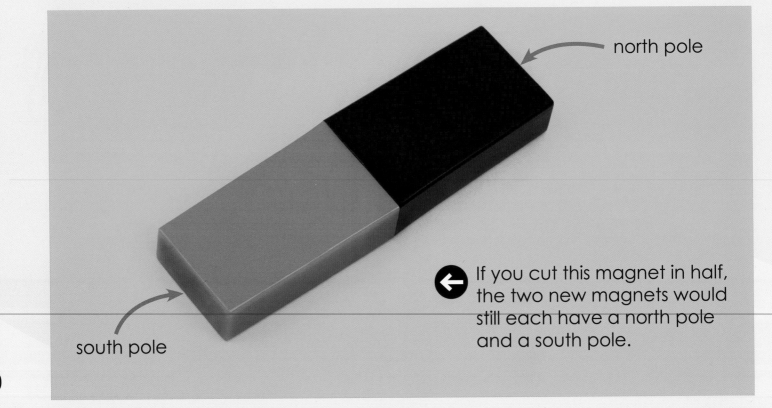

north pole

south pole

If you cut this magnet in half, the two new magnets would still each have a north pole and a south pole.

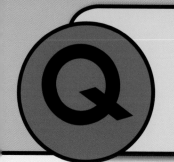
CLUE

- What is the opposite of pull?

The south pole of one magnet pushes away the south pole of another magnet. It **repels** the other magnet.

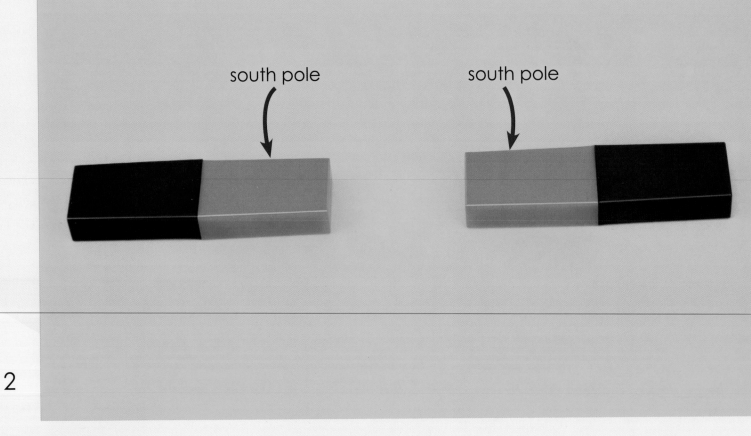

south pole

south pole

The north pole of one magnet will also repel the north pole of another magnet. Opposite poles attract. Poles that are alike repel each other.

This toy uses magnets.

How Strong Are Magnets?

A magnet can only pull objects that are inside its **magnetic field**. The magnetic field is the distance that a magnet's pull can reach. A magnet pulls most strongly at its **poles**.

 The iron filings around this magnet show its magnetic field. There are more filings at the ends of the magnet because this is where the pull is strongest.

The further the magnet is away from the paper clips, the less able it is to pull them.

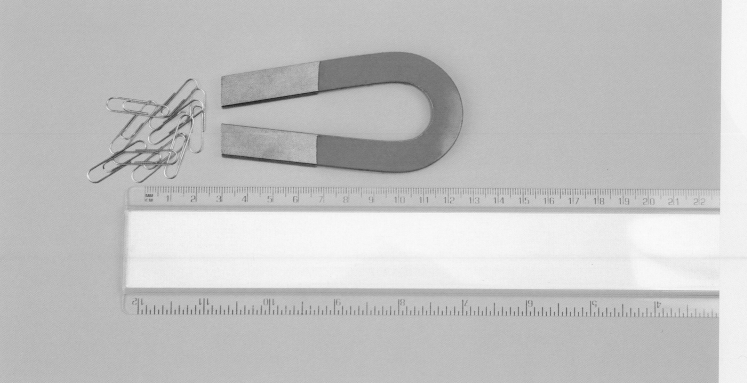

The pull is strongest when objects are close to the magnet. When objects are farther away, it is harder for the magnet to pull them.

Some magnets have a stronger **magnetic field** than others. A magnet cannot pull objects that are too far away.

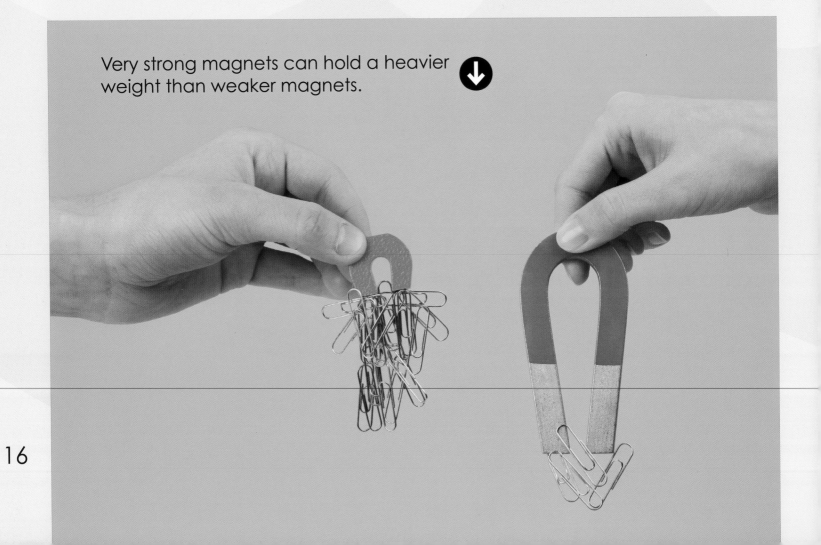

Very strong magnets can hold a heavier weight than weaker magnets.

Q What happens if you put something in between a magnet and a magnetic object?

CLUE

- How do people use refrigerator magnets?

A A magnet can **attract** objects through other materials, such as paper. The magnetic pull can travel through other materials. But if the magnet is too weak, the magnetic pull will not reach through the other material.

This frog magnet can hold this sheet of paper against a refrigerator.

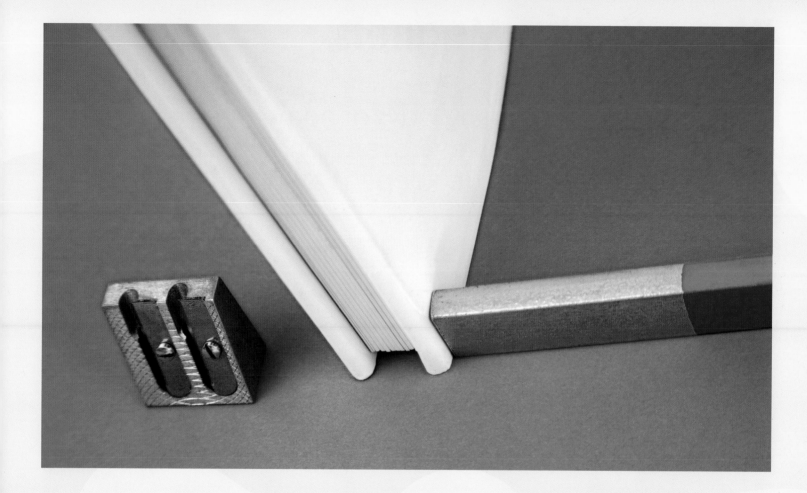

If the material in between is too thick, the magnetic pull will not reach an iron object. If you put too many pieces of paper under a refrigerator magnet, it will fall off the refrigerator.

Ways We Use Magnets

We use magnets in many ways at home. The doors on refrigerators, microwave ovens, and freezers have magnets around them to keep the door shut tightly.

Many toys use magnets. There are magnets in some can openers and screwdrivers. There are even magnets in electric motors, CD players, computers, and telephones.

This fishing game uses magnets to pick up fish.

Magnets can be used to sort garbage. A large magnet **attracts** the iron and steel so it can be used again or **recycled**.

High-speed trains use magnets. There are magnets on the train and in the track that **repel** each other. This makes the train float above the track, so the ride is less bumpy. This means it can travel faster.

People use a magnetic **compass** to find the right direction. People use a magnetic compass when they are hiking.

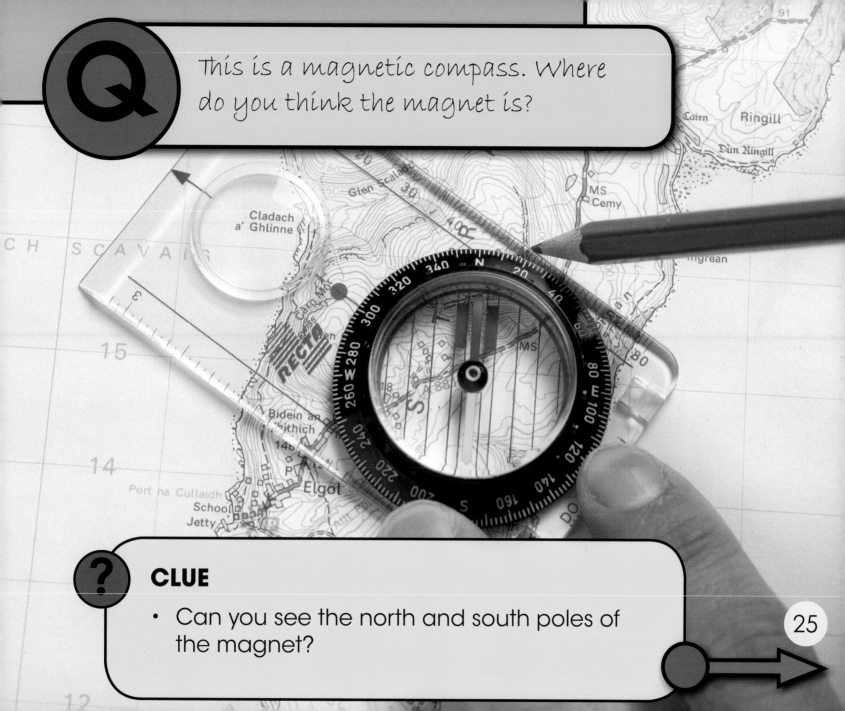

Q This is a magnetic compass. Where do you think the magnet is?

? **CLUE**

- Can you see the north and south poles of the magnet?

The needle on the compass is a magnet. The needle shows us which way is north. This helps us to find the right direction.

needle

Magnetic compasses work because the core (center) of Earth is magnetic. There is hot melted iron in Earth's core.

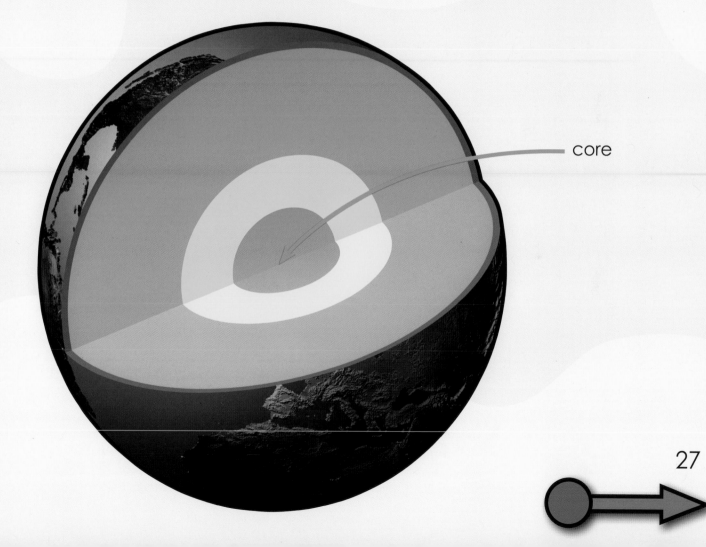

core

Some animals have a **magnetic sense**. This sense helps them to find the right direction.

↑ Migrating birds use their magnetic sense to find their way.

Magnets are amazing! We use them all the time in our lives. Scientists are finding new ways to use magnets all the time. Do you use anything that is magnetic?

Doctors use machines with magnets in to find out what is wrong with their patients.

Checklist

 ➠ A magnet can pull toward **(attract)** other magnets.

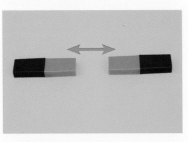 ➠ A magnet can also push away **(repel)** other magnets.

 ➠ A magnet can attract some metals, including iron, steel, and nickel.

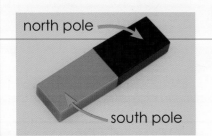 ➠ A magnet has a north **pole** and a south pole.

north pole

south pole

Glossary

attract pull towards

compass tool used to find the right direction

force push or pull

magnetic field distance that a magnet's pull can reach

magnetic sense special sense some animals have to find their way

magnetism force that magnets use

poles opposite ends or sides of a magnet

recycle use again

repel push away

Index